IMAGES OF
THANET

BARRIE WOOTTON

POST BAW CARD

FOR INLAND USE ONLY
THIS SPACE MAY BE USED
FOR COMMUNICATION

Any Photograph will be
copied, or a New Portrait
may be taken and printed
as actual Photographic
Post Cards, at

3/6 per dozen.

Suitable Mottoes on the
front side.

Ask to see Specimens, at
the Studio.

THE ADDRESS ONLY TO 69
WRITTEN HERE

Christmas Post Cards.

Actual Photographs.

SWAINE,

Photographer,
Broadstairs.

THE PHOTOGRAPHS OF THOMAS PAGE SWAINE

SUTTON PUBLISHING

Sutton Publishing Limited
Phoenix Mill · Thrupp · Stroud
Gloucestershire · GL5 2BU

First published 2004

Copyright © Barrie Wootton, 2004

Title page: It pays to advertise: an
advertisement for Thomas P. Swaine's
photographic work.

British Library Cataloguing in Publication Data
A catalogue record for this book is available from the
British Library.

ISBN 0-7509-4034-4

Typeset in 10.5/13.5 Photina.
Typesetting and origination by
Sutton Publishing Limited.
Printed and bound in England by
J.H. Haynes & Co. Ltd, Sparkford.

> *This book is dedicated to Joan Ingledew (née Swaine),*
> *Thomas P. Swaine's only granddaughter, and her husband Bob,*
> *who have encouraged, supported and waited so long*
> *for this publication.*

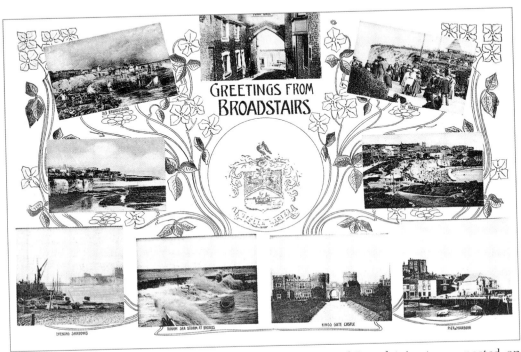

A Swaine postcard of Broadstairs showing multi-views of Broadstairs town, posted on
21 August 1907 to 85 Rue de Bennes, Paris, France.

CONTENTS

Local boarding houses would pay the princely sum of 16s 8d for 100 postcards of their illustrious establishment to hand out to visitors.

Thomas Page Swaine
(b. 11 September 1864; d. 11 June 1923)

INTRODUCTION

Thomas Page Swaine's photographic skills captured Victorian and Edwardian Thanet, as well as the local personalities who helped to give the island its special place in the hearts of residents and visitors alike. His photographic talent touched on areas as diverse as Thanet (particularly Broadstairs), Folkestone, Canterbury and Sturry. Although his stay in Broadstairs was only twelve years, the sights he recorded with his camera are unique, and give us an insight into the events in peoples lives and the changes that have occurred in the three towns of Broadstairs, Ramsgate and Margate.

Through the medium of the humble postcard, costing then 1*d*, Thomas has given us the chance to turn back the clock 100 years, and stare at the faces and places of people of that era. How simple and uncomplicated their lives were. Thomas Swaine has forever captured their images.

The story does not stop there, because Thomas's eldest son Ernest and his brother Stanley also later followed their father's profession of photography. Indeed, Ernest opened a shop in Broadstairs High Street in 1947, and I also include some of Ernest's photographs here. One or two of Stanley's photographs are included because of their historic significance to the Royal Navy's Fleet Air Arm.

Thomas's only daughter Doris did not become a photographer, but worked long hours in the family's shop and married late in life. The only member of the family to escape photography altogether was Albert Lewis Bradstowe Swaine, who after the the First World War went off to Malaya and became a successful rubber planter.

So sit back and enjoy a slice of nostalgia by courtesy of Thomas Page Swaine and family.

Broadstairs High Street, *c*. 1900. On the right is Thomas P. Swaine's shop. Perhaps the lady and girl are about to have their photograph taken by Mr Swaine, and are taking the opportunity to choose a frame.

ACKNOWLEDGEMENTS

Firstly, I am indebted to Dot Toft for her shared interest whether typing, proof reading or helping in constructing the text and layout of this book. My special thanks must also go to the people who have assisted me with the gathering of research material namely John Williams, Mick Twyman, Don Dimond, Derek and Alan Butler, Ann and Peter Hooper and George Gosling. To the many friends and members of the Canterbury & East Kent Postcard Club who have lent a sympathetic ear or directed me to many rare postcards, my grateful appreciation.

Here I must give a special mention to Clive Baker, friend and postcard dealer who has unearthed many Swaine postcards in his travels. I also owe very special thanks to Brian Gilham of St Peter's Park Road, Broadstairs, who finally revealed where Thomas P. Swaine's family could be found, after my vain searches over many years.

In addition, thanks go to Cliff Cole of the Isle of Thanet Family History Society who kindly located the birthplace of Thomas. I would also like to record here my sincere thanks and appreciation to the staff at Ramsgate, Broadstairs and Margate libraries.

Finally, I would like to acknowledge the time spent by Joan and Bob Ingledew in imparting family memories during their annual visits to Broadstairs, and the encouragement they have shown, which I have thoroughly enjoyed.

If I have inadvertently infringed any copyright or omitted names of the many people who have pointed out or added information to this quest of Thomas P. Swaine's life and times, my sincere apologies.

Of course, I must not forget my dear wife's patience, forebearance and support during the many hours I have spent on this ongoing obsession! Lastly, to readers of this book, I must say there are still many unanswered questions on this man's life. If you know anything else, I would very much appreciate hearing from you.

1

Early Family Days

Thomas Page Swaine's eldest son, Ernest
Horace Swaine, born on Wednesday
11 February 1891.

On Sunday 11 September 1864 a son named Thomas was born to a fisherman, Thomas Page Swaine, and his wife Rachel, née Spice, at their home, 1 Winding Street, in the parish of St Clement in the town of Hastings, Sussex.

Little is known of Thomas's early life. In the 1881 census he is shown as living with his grandparents, William and Sarah Spice, still at 1 Winding Street. There is no mention of his parents and his age is given as 16. Thomas's profession was recorded as photography.

The next information we have about Thomas relates to his marriage at St Paul's Church, Sandgate, on Thursday 29 May 1890 to Jessie Alice Box. Thomas was 25; his bride, aged 21, was the daughter of Edwin Box, a draper in Folkestone. Over the next twelve years there followed four children, and some of Thomas's most happy and eventful years.

The couple's first son, Ernest, was born at Oundle Villa, Priory Hill, Charlton, Dover, in 1891. Two years later he moved with his parents to Broadstairs. Here, Thomas became the manager of Mr Houghton's shop at 17 High Street in Broadstairs, and after two years in this managerial position he decided to set up his own photographic business in St Peter's. The decision to start his own business was a sound idea, but either Thomas had forgotten, or chose to ignore, an agreement with Houghton that he would not set up a rival business in the same district.

So when Thomas opened his business in St Peter's, under 2 miles from where he formerly worked, he was promptly sued by Houghton and had to pay his former employer £100 plus £50 costs. Thomas was out of work for nine months, and then an arrangement was made between Dr Barlow, Charles Higgs and Thomas to purchase Mr Houghton's business for £400. This sum included the £100 already owed by Thomas. Thomas was to be manager, with a salary of £3 a week, and would repay the £400 as and when he could at 4 per cent interest. The business was known as Swaine & Co., Broadstairs, and for a time was quite successful, although none of the money was repaid.

In 1898 Thomas leased larger premises at 41 High Street. Disaster then struck his amicable agreement with Messrs Barlow and Higgs. Dr Barlow was taken seriously ill and the debt was called in. Borrowing again, this time from H.H. Marks, Thomas began the struggle to repay his debt.

In 1903, the year after his daughter Doris was born, tragedy was to befall the family business again. In the early hours of Friday 27 November a serious fire broke out in the basement of 41 High Street, Thomas's home and shop. His family was at home, as well as his wife Jessie's sister and a servant, but Thomas saw everyone to safety and raised the alarm. Both Broadstairs and Ramsgate fire brigades were needed before the fire was finally put out at 7.40 a.m. Thomas suffered the loss of the basement (his workshop), the shop and top room, including most of his furniture. In their haste to evacuate the premises, the family's pet dog was forgotten, and was later found dead.

More troubles were to follow. Thomas later reported that he had returned to the blazing building to retrieve his cash box and ledgers, and having saved these items handed them to a man standing across the road who promised to look after them. On returning to retrieve them later, Thomas found the man and the cash box missing. Sadly, his problems did not end there. Thomas was under-insured, and so was unable to replace his equipment and stock.

The Swaine family found temporary accommodation in John Street, but Thomas was out of work for three or four months. When he revived his business there was competition from another photographer. Furthermore, the introduction of cameras that could be bought by the public begun to make inroads into his profits. When he first started in photography, portraits cost £2 2s (2 guineas) each. By 1910 the price of a photograph was down to 3s 6d per dozen. The result was that in 1911 Thomas was declared bankrupt. The outcome of this has yet to be discovered, but for two years he was not recorded as being in business. Then in 1913 a photographic company called Beaulah & Swaine was recorded at West Cliff Studio, 6 Royal Road, West Cliff, Ramsgate. Research over the years has failed to produce any evidence of anyone named Beaulah, but this is definitely our Thomas Page Swaine.

In 1920 Beaulah & Swaine disappeared from local directories and no trace can be found of the name Swaine in Thanet. I have discovered, however, through Thomas P. Swaine's only granddaughter, Joan Ingledew, that Thomas moved to Bedford during 1917, starting another photographic business in Bedford High Street. His home was in Waterloo Road, and it was here on Monday 11 June 1923 that he died of cancer, aged 58.

In the following pages you will be able to judge for yourself how good a photographer Thomas Page Swaine was: with the exception of approximately ten photographs, everything is his own work. I hope you enjoy the fruits of his labours.

Young Ernest Swaine (second from left) with his father Thomas P. Swaine (second from the right) in this line up of Ye Old Bradstowe Clubbe of Wheelers, or Broadstairs Cycling Club, 1901.

Albert Lewis Bradstowe Swaine, OBE, EC, born on Sunday 25 October 1896. Albert is the officer in the centre of the front row. He was the second son of Thomas and the first to be born in Broadstairs, hence his middle name of Bradstowe, the old name for Broadstairs.

nley Eric Gordon Swaine was born on
April 1898. Stanley was Thomas's third
1. He went on to create a career as a
otographer in the Royal Air Force, no
ibt having been trained by his father as a
y. He too, like his brother, was born at the
w business premises of 41 High Street,
oadstairs. This photograph shows Stanley
 the extreme left relaxing with the Swaine
nily while on leave at their home in
arlotte Street, Bedford.

ris Gwendoline Bertha Swaine, born on
ursday 29 May 1902. The last child and
ly daughter of Thomas Swaine, for many
ars she worked and helped in her father's
isiness before marrying late in life and
coming Mrs Newman.

Broadstairs Fire Brigade. *c.* 1900. Some of these firemen would have been responsible for putting the f[...] out at the Swaine shop in the High Street in 1903.

Opposite: In 1903 Thomas became the Worshipful Master of the Masons Lodge in Broadstairs. This is the menu card of his installation into the office. Life certainly had its ups and downs for him.

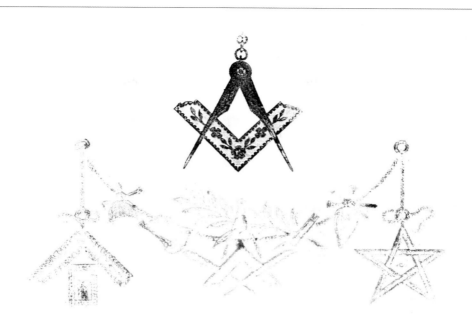

BRADSTOW LODGE,

No. 2448.

Installation Banquet,

SEPTEMBER 23RD, 1903.

Bro. THOS. P. SWAINE,

Worshipful Master.

Menu and Toast List

An early *carte de visite* portrait of a young woman. When this photograph was taken, good money could be made out of photography, then only in its infancy.

A view of a walking race in Ramsgate, *c.* 1913.

2

St Peter's & Reading Street

The funeral of the Revd Alfred Whitehead, 21 March 1898.
Alfred Whitehead was Vicar of St Peter's Church from
1871 to 1898, and was responsible for a number of
restoration projects at the church. The building on the
extreme left is the old public house The Wheatsheaf.
(by kind permission of Mrs Sally Wood, verger,
St Peter's Church)

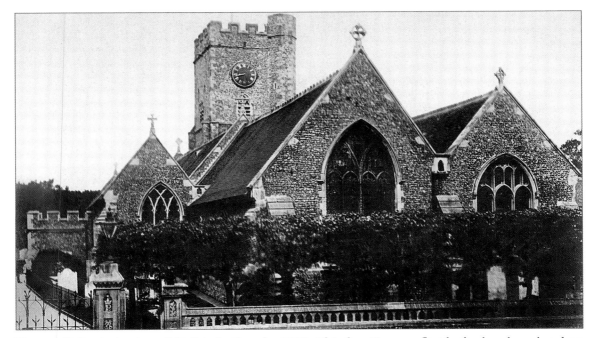

Thomas P. Swaine's view of St Peter's Church, 1900. This fine Norman flint-built church replaced an early Saxon wooden edifice built on the site. The clock depicted on the tower was built by William Vale of London in 1802, with the installation carried out by a carpenter and bricklayer at a total cost of £103.

An early interior view of St Peter's Church showing the very ornate ceiling, which is transfer printed. Mrs Noot of Upton Lodge replaced the east window seen here in the 1920s as a dedication to her young son Mervyn, who was killed on 20 October 1914 at Radinghem Wood. Second Lieutenant Noot was serving with the East Kent Regiment of 'the Buffs' during the First World War.

St Peter's High Street, *c.* 1905. This view shows on the left the old Crown and Thistle public house. Owned by the local Ramsgate Brewery of Thomson & Wotton, the pub dated back to the eighteenth century. It closed in 1954, but was not finally pulled down until 1960 when the road was widened. Two modern shops, set back, now occupy the site.

This delightful rural scene is Sowell Street Farm. Now sadly gone, it was situated at the St Peter's Park Road end of Sowell Street on the left hand side. In the 1900s George Nutting was the farm bailiff; he ran the farm for Edward Stephen Goodson of Upton Farm.

Sowell Street farmyard seen here was next to St Peter's Court Preparatory School. The school was attended by the Dukes of Kent and Gloucester. In 1913 they were visited by their mother and father, King George V and Queen Mary. Another notable pupil was the present Lord Montagu of Beaulieu.

Mr Edmund Davis, who lived in St Peter's Cottage in Sowell Street (sadly demolished). He was a millionaire and paid for the laying out of the gardens in front of the Granville Hotel, Ramsgate.

e Isle of Thanet Tramways staff, 1901. The picture was taken outside the main depot at the bottom of rthdown Hill, St Peter's. The trams ran from 3 April 1901 until 24 March 1937. The tenth man from left in the second row is thought to be Mr Murphy, who engineered the building of the tramways and ne from Ireland.

e White Swan public house, known to some as the 'Mucky Duck', 1910. This was another Thomson Wotton hostelry. In 1913 the brewery demolished this eighteenth-century building and built the pub know today. There was once another pub in Trinity Square called 'the North Star'. This was closed wn because of its smuggling connections, and finally burnt down on 22 July 1909.

Sleepy Reading Street. On the right is Lawrence Terr
followed by the post office and grocery store owned
Mr Johnson (known to the villagers as 'Diddly Johns
and then 'Wellbeck Terrace'. The postcard was poste
21 October 1904 (Trafalgar Day) and sent to Miss E
Sharp, Yarrow Home, Broadstairs, which is now
Broadstairs Technical College.

Entitled 'An old Farmhouse Nr. Broadstairs', this pic
is of the White Swan Cottage in Reading Street next
the public house. Here, the famous 'Waterloo' or 'Je
cabbage grew in the garden. The cabbage grew to 2
high, and its stalks could be used for rafters in thatc
roofs or as walking sticks. The leaves when fed to co
sheep improved the quality of the milk and the woo

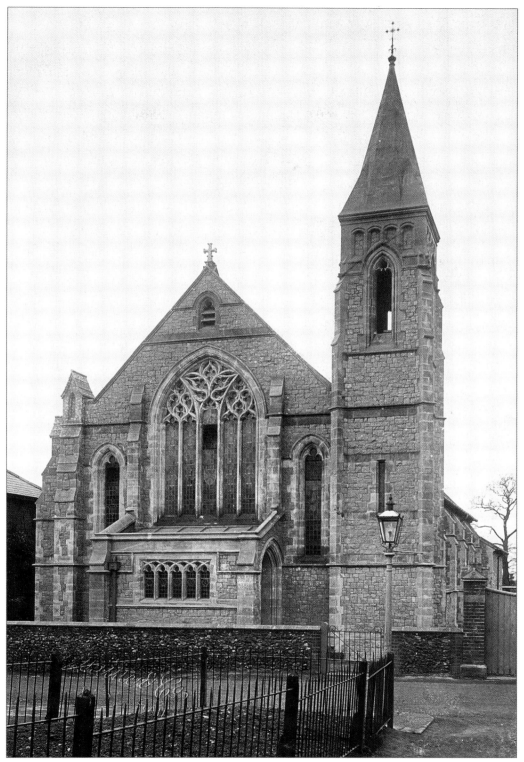

St Andrew's Church, Reading Street. Built on land that was once a farm belonging to Rimpton Court, the church was consecrated by the Archbishop of Canterbury on 10 April 1911. The only other place of worship open to villagers was a Baptist chapel on the corner of Trinity Square (now demolished).

Elmwood House, situated at the junction of Reading Street, Elmwood Avenue and Callis Court Road was Tudor built, and in 1801 Sir James Fisher took up residence there. The most famous resident associated with this house is not Sir James but Alfred Harmsworth, later Lord Northcliffe, as founder of the popular newspaper the *Daily Mail* and owner, with his brother, of the *Evening News*. He bought Elmwood in 1889, spent two years modernising his retreat and finally moved in in 1891. Incidentally, Alfred Harmsworth didn't learn to read until the age of seven. During the First World War he became Minister for Propaganda

The extensive gardens of Elmwood took five gardeners to look after them. Some were housed in the Bothey, known today as Gardenia Cottage, in the grounds of Elmwood House. Elmwood has another claim to fame in that Douglas Fairbanks Senior and Mary Pickford spent their secret honeymoon at Elmwood Cottage as the guests of Alfred Harmsworth, after they married in 1920. They were the biggest film stars of silent movie days.

is large ornamental pond in the grounds of
nwood' was believed to contain an alligator!
ere is a reference to this on the back of the
stcard depicted here.

is postcard shows the flowerbed in front of the
nadian farmhouse built for Lord Northcliffe,
hin the grounds of Elmwood. Many connections
h Broadstairs and St Peter's were forged with
· Harmsworths. For example, in 1910 the 1st
padstairs Scout Troop became known as Lady
rthcliffe's own Regiment of Scouts. Thomas
idd, the scoutmaster, was Headmaster of Holy
nity School locally known as Tommy Studd's
ademy.

Elmwood Cottages, now demolished. These cottages once belonged to Josse Farm, later named Elmwood Farm, and stood in the field opposite Elmwood House, Callis Court Road. They became part of the Northcliffe Estate along with the farm. Once again, Thomas P. Swaine has posed his wife and daughter in this picture.

Callis Court, the magnificent holiday home of Harry Hanoel Marks, MP for Thanet. The inkblot on the tower to the left marks the room where a young French girl named Blanche was staying. She sent this souvenir of 'La Chateau of Deputes' to her friend in France. It is believed that Marks purchased Callis Court from Mr Richard Potter in 1889, and after the death of his wife Estelle it was sold by public auction in 1916.

H.H. Marks, MP and JP for Thanet, owner and editor of the *Financial News*, the first solely financial newspaper of its day. He was born in London on 9 April 1855.

The entrance to Josse Gap, *c*. 1900. This entrance on to the sands of Joss Bay takes its name from the family of Josse, who owned the farm at the top of Elmwood Road and the surrounding land in Queen Elizabeth I's reign. The Josse family made the gap so that they could harvest the seaweed as manure for their fields. The infamous smuggler Joss Snelling took his name from this bay.

A view from the seaward side of Joss Gap, an ideal area for the smugglers to ply their trade in the eighteenth century. What a dark and lonely place this must have been in those days. In 1905 this wooden barrier prevented any commercial business being carried out, as the area was private. Any brakes taking sightseers around could rest only at designated stops such as the Lighthouse, Captain Digby or North Foreland Teahouse.

A Scout camp at Joss Bay, July 1909. Permission would have been sought and granted before even a tent peg touched the grass. Broadstairs and St Peter's Urban District Council purchased the foreshore of Kinsgate, Botany and Whiteness for £2,000 in 1933, because it was feared Margate would purchase the area – and that daytrippers would ruin its peace and tranquillity. Incidentally, the foreshore rights to Joss Bay were purchased much later as in 1933 the asking price was £20,000.

Kingsgate Castle, erected in 1763, was one of Lord Holland's most spectacular follies. Thomas Wynne built this castle as a coach house and servants' quarters for the nearby Holland House, which had been built in 1761.

Kingsgate Castle was bought in 1900 by Lord Avebury, who enlarged it considerably. He is better known as Sir John Lubbock, who introduced the Bank Holiday Act which was passed by Parliament in 1871. Lord Avebury died at Kingsgate Castle in 1913. The late Bill Lapthorne, a noted local historian, tells us that the castle was built on the site of a Tudor farmhouse.

Kingsgate Bay looking towards the Captain Digby. On the left are the gardens for Holland House and the coastguard cottages. The Digby is all that remains of a bede house, which in 1813 was demolished after a violent storm, leaving only the stables – today's Captain Digby public house & restaurant.

This view taken in the other direction, shows numerous buildings built for Lord Holland. All of these buildings have a purpose, apart from the small tower. From right to left, they are the Captain Digby, a small tower, Little Holland House, Holland House, Kingsgate Castle and the Countess Tower.

Arx Ruochim, originally called Innis Ruochim. This is a replica of Henry VIII's fort built at Deal. The tower in the centre is built of chalk blocks; it has now collapsed. Legend has it that the tower marks King Vortigern's grave, but there is nothing to substantiate this myth. The central tower was once thought to be Neptune's Tower but early maps indicate that this was in a totally different place.

Kingsgate Gap, 1905. This gap between the cliffs no longer looks as it is depicted on this postcard. Erosion of the chalk has seen the arch and cliff to the right totally disappear. Again, Jessie Swaine and daughter Doris pose for the camera.

Leon's Cottage was situated on the Cliff Promenade, North Foreland (note the lighthouse in the background). In 1905, it was the home of Mr W. Crawford. Leon's Cottage was also a rest home; the matron was Mr Crawford's wife.

North Foreland Lighthouse was the last manned lighthouse in Great Britain. This particular building dates from 1691, but there were earlier beacons going back to Roman times. In 1900 the Marconi Company opened a wireless station at North Foreland. It was run by one man, a William Watson for six months. Later the post office took over the station and transferred it to a house opposite the lighthouse, placing Mr Oglivey in charge. In 1928 he moved to Rumfields along with the radio station. His daughter, Mrs Connie Taylor, still lives in St Peter's.

A Swaine photographic postcard of the North Foreland Tea House, better known as the Dutch Tea House. It is situated on the east side of North Foreland Road. It was a popular stop for horse-drawn brakes in the early 1900s.

Printed by an unknown publisher, this postcard depicts the interior of the North Foreland Tea House. In the bottom left-hand corner can be seen the words 'Swaine Photo Broadstairs'. Thomas Swaine must have sold the copyright.

St Winifred's School, situated on the Cliff Promenade, North Foreland. This private school was for young ladies only. Sadly, I can find no trace of this fine establishment today. Certainly it was still around in the 1920s, as there are postcards depicting the school's outdoor lessons and Guides pack in the grounds. I would very much like to hear from anyone who has memories of this school.

Stone House, *c.* 1905. This house has a long and chequered history. It was built in 1764 for Sir Charles Raymond and later became the residence of Archbishop Tait, Archbishop of Canterbury. The Archbishop gave 5 acres of ground to build the Tait Orphanage and Convalescent Home. Later Stone House became a preparatory school and is now a listed building, divided into private apartments.

North Foreland viewed from the newly developed Eastern Esplanade, 1895. Note the lack of housing on the horizon. Among those well-known people to have property built on this sought-after headland were Sir Robert McAlpine and Lord Lawrence of Kingsgate. The last building on the esplanade is the Wainwright Convalescent Home for Children, built in 1891.

3

Broadstairs Eastern Esplanade

St John's House of Rest was on the Eastern Esplanade. It was built as a holiday home for clerics and had a Sister Eleanor in charge. This beautiful building was demolished along with St Mary's children's home in the late 1960s.

Thomas P. Swaine's portrait of Mr. F.E. McCormick Goodhart of Langley Lodge, Eastern
Esplanade. Goodhart was a Conservative and Unionist candidate in the 1904 election. Langley
Lodge later became Cliffcoombe Nursing Home, where in 1933 Dolly Irving, the wife of Sir
Henry Irving, the great Victorian actor, died.

Joseph King, Liberal candidate for the 1904 Election & political opponent to McCormick Goodhart & H.H. Marks. An early voting slogan used by Marks, the successful Candidate, was 'Vote for Marks with Goodhart & No Joe King'.

Mascotte is the name of this fine boarding house, seen here in 1908. It was supervised by the Misses Brown and Hopkins and was situated next door to Mr McCormick Goodhart's residence on the Eastern Esplanade. The message on the reverse of this postcard was from Beatie Carpenter to a Mrs Read of Petersfield, Hampshire. This fine building has been demolished along with the other beautiful Victorian houses that once graced this promenade.

St Mary's Convalescent Home for Children on the Eastern Esplanade, Broadstairs, built at a cost of £60,000 by the Sisters of Kilburn. The home was opened by the Princesses Christian and Frederica of Hanover in July 1887. This postcard is unique in that it shows half of the Swaine family. The boy by the barrow is Ernest Swaine, the eldest son, and the lady is Jessie Swaine, with baby Doris in the pram.

St Mary's from Stone Road. This view shows the only entrance to the convalescent home's grounds. To gain the sands of Stone Bay below the cliffs, a tunnel was dug from the grounds through the cliffs – so children didn't have to cross a road to get to the sands. The entrance to the tunnel on the sands can still be seen today, but the tunnel itself has been filled in.

A view of 5 Dickens Road, Broadstairs, owned by Henry W. Fussell in November 1914 when this card was posted to Albert of Mess 32 HM *Superb*, and the house no. 5 was known as Coniscliffe at this time. I wonder what happened to Albert.

Clevedon Hotel on the Eastern Esplanade. For many years the Invalid Children's Aid Association occupied this building, with Miss D. Hacking as Matron. In a message on the reverse of this postcard, Maurice Vincent of Salisbury told his mum he thought 'Broadstairs a lovely place'. The hotel has since been demolished and Copperfield Court stands on this site. Broadstairs is still a lovely place!

Depicted here in its original state, Fort House was built in 1801 for a Captain Gooch, who was in command of a small fort situated in front of the house. In 1851 Charles Dickens, the famous author, first took up residence. He dearly loved the house and penned many of his novels in these quiet hallowed rooms. The house subsequently changed its name to Bleak House, after one of his famous books.

Bleak House in 1905, after the resident owner, Mr Barry, had extended and castellated the whole building. The result, as can be seen, completely changed the character of the building. Dickens, I am sure, would not have been impressed, but may well have been amused when Mr Barry was declared bankrupt in later years.

Bleak House overlooking the houses of Cosy Nook. The Victorian wooden breakwaters were an early attempt to prevent King Neptune's realm from sweeping away the cliffs of Albion.

Holy Trinity Church, Broadstairs, was originally known as Bradstowe Chapel and was built on ground belonging to Bleak House. At a cost of £300, the tower was added in 1862. This flimsy construction was eventually pulled down in the 1920s and the body of the church was enlarged.

The interior of Holy Trinity Church, in 1905. The church was a chapel of ease to St Peter's before the town of Broadstairs was made a separate parish in 1856. Charles Dickens, on first seeing Bradstowe Chapel, likened it to a 'petrified haystack', harsh words perhaps.

The Chalet, a rather large house in Rectory Road built on ground that was once part of the Bleak House estate. One wonders why Thomas P. Swaine took so many photographs of individual premises, but perhaps they were sold to visitors who stayed there on holiday.

Another view of the Chalet. On the right of the building in the background can be seen Holy Trinity Rectory, built in 1871, and the old church tower. Parked in front of the house is a piece of Victorian ingenuity, a large tricycle: is this for man or boy, I wonder?

4

The Old Pier & Sands

As the title suggests, this view is taken from Bleak House and shows a quiet day on the sands. On the horizon, few houses can be seen on the Western Esplanade, which was not developed until the late 1920s. Marsh's bathing machines can be seen spread along the beach, and in the left foreground a Thames barge is being unloaded by horse and cart.

Broadstairs Pier after the storm of 1897. The pier was almost demolished. This Swaine photograph was used by the *London Illustrated News* in an article on the storm's effects on the south-east coast.

Broadstairs Pier restored to its former glory, *c.* 1905. The view shows how the old pier has changed over the years. Today's car park on the seaward side of the pier did not exist. It is small wonder that the early postcards showed masses of seawater rushing over the pier. Its width was half of what it is today. The lifeboat on the end of the pier is the *Francis Forbes Barton*.

he pier awash in rough weather. This postcard was posted on 25 August 1905 to Miss E. Wallace of
2 Alexander Road, Broadstairs.

A much calmer day, showing the old Tartar Frigate public house on the far left. The old look-out house, whose loft doors can be seen open, housed sails, oars and other articles for the fishermen's wherries. In 1881 Solomon Holbourne was appointed harbourmaster for the princely sum of 30s a week.

A busy day in Broadstairs harbour: three Thames sailing barges are being unloaded. These barges were regular visitors as they transported coal to the town's gasworks. They often loaded lime and tar in their holds for their return journey.

Another view of the harbour, showing the sands at high tide. Various fishing vessels can be seen moored here. In past times Broadstairs fishermen fished for cod on the banks of Newfoundland, Canada. The local industry of manufacturing cod liver oil was renowned.

telescopic view of the harbour, created Thomas P. Swaine.

This view shows some of the oldest and most interesting buildings connected with Broadstairs history. From left to right: Eagle House, Eldon Place, the Auction Rooms of Rennolls & Childs, Bleak House and York Gate House. A new roof is being installed at the Alexandra 6*d* Bazaar.

The walled-in ground shown here once belonged to White's Shipyard; it later became a
bowling green and is now the site of the popular Broadstairs Pavilion.

Mr Wilson's Bathing Tents seen here, were situated on the sands between the main steps and York Ga
steps. There were not many bathing costumes on show when Thomas P. Swaine took this photograp

...nich is a far cry from today's scantily clad bathers. When this photograph was taken, it was regarded residents and Council alike that bathing after 1 p.m. was anti-social!

he main bay sands, crowded near the sea edge, are virtually deserted near the cliffs. J.G. Marsh's
athing Machines vie for business with the bathing tents, owned by Mr Wilson, which would later oust
ae bathing machines. The bay was subsequently renamed Viking Bay in honour of the successful
augural landing of the Viking ship, *Hugin*, on 28 July 1949.

posite, above: Broadstairs main bay, early 1900s. This postcard is entitled 'Afternoon Shadows' and you
a almost see the quietness. There are only two houses visible on the Western Esplanade, with the
ckmaster Home (built in 1895 for Ladies in Distress) located between them and the Grand Hotel.

posite, below: Broadstairs Old Pier dates back to 1490. The shrimper is already at work and the
adowy outline of the lifeboat can be seen poised on the pier.

The sands from Preacher's Knoll, 1905. These crowded golden sands and sheltered bay still give many happy hours to today's children as they did in their great grandparents' day.

e bay from the opposite direction. The sands are not so crowded. Houses are clustered around
e clifftop, while beyond are open fields. How Broadstairs has grown since 1905 when this card
s posted, with the advent of tourism during the 1920s and '30s.

The Sunday School Union holds a service on the sands under the shadow of the aptly named Preacher's Knoll, 4 April 1905.

Broadstairs main bay, late 1890s. This postcard is a complete mystery to me. There seems to be no report of this incident in any local publications. Thomas P. Swaine did not come to Broadstairs until 1893, so when did this incident occur?

A coloured Swaine postcard, one of only two in my entire collection, this view centres on the two Thames barges of A.H. Keep and the old lifeboat seen on the end of the pier. These barges were often the victims of bad weather, their crews' only salvation being the small lifeboat shown here and its brave crew.

5

Broadstairs Lifeboats

The crew and locals pose for Thomas P. Swaine by the second RNLI lifeboat,
Christopher Waud Bradford. The lifeboat is on the old wooden slipway, built by a local
Norwegian, Olaf Johnson, for the princely sum of £98.

Broadstairs' lifeboat crew posing for Thomas P. Swaine around the old look-out and storehouse at the beginning of the pier, 1905.

other posed photograph depicts the *Francis Forbes Barton* and her crew about to be launched. This last
adstairs lifeboat was towed away for a refit in 1912 never to return, and the Broadstairs station was
sed. Surprisingly, this boat still exists and is being repaired at Littlehampton, West Sussex.

Above: The quarterly exercise of the Broadstairs lifeboat, 1910. Thomas P. Swaine took this photograph from the slipway at the end of Broadstairs Pier. The *Francis Forbes Barton* was 'on station' for fifteen years and in that time saved 115 lives.

Right: The Broadstairs RNLI station existed from 1886 when the first lifeboat, the *Samuel Morrison Collins*, came 'on station', until the *Francis Forbes Barton* left Broadstairs in 1912. In that time 269 lives were saved. The message on the reverse of this postcard sums up the feeling of Broadstairs folk at the loss of their lifeboat: 'Opposite Louisa Gap, Broadstairs, this barge sank on the morning of April 12th 1913. Crew saved by Ramsgate Lifeboat, Broadstairs having no lifeboat.'

Left: The silver medal that was presented to Lifeboatman William Wales on behalf of the President of the United States of America, James Buchanan, for his part in rescuing the crew of the *Northern Bell* off Kingsgate in 1857. William Wales was one of the crew of the Broadstairs lifeboats *Culmer White*, which along with the *Mary White* had to be manhandled from Broadstairs to Kingsgate before effecting the rescue; this was carried out during snow and hailstone blizzards. William Wales was born in Northwood in 1823 and joined the lifeboat crew after serving in the Royal Navy, finally dying at the ripe old age of 91 in 1914.

6

The Broadstairs
Entertainers

Uncle Mack's Minstrels. I doubt if there is another entertainer in England who could equal the record of J.H. Summerson, known to Broadstairs residents and visitors alike as Uncle Mack. He was the subject of many postcards produced by Thomas P. Swaine during his years at Broadstairs. Mac was busking with his friend Fred Hawley in 1895 on Broadstairs Promenade. Later that same year he joined Uncle Ned's Mowhawk Minstrels, simply known as Mack, but in 1900 he took on the mantle of Uncle Mack and his Minstrels. Fred Hawley became one of these first minstrels and took up permanent residence in Broadstairs. Uncle Mack only ever missed one season in the next forty-eight years, apart from the interruption of the First and Second World Wars. The year missed was 1905, when Broadstairs Pier and Harbour Commissioners accepted the lower tender from Broadstairs Merry Mascots. The following year 1906, saw Uncle Mack and his Minstrels return, never to leave again.

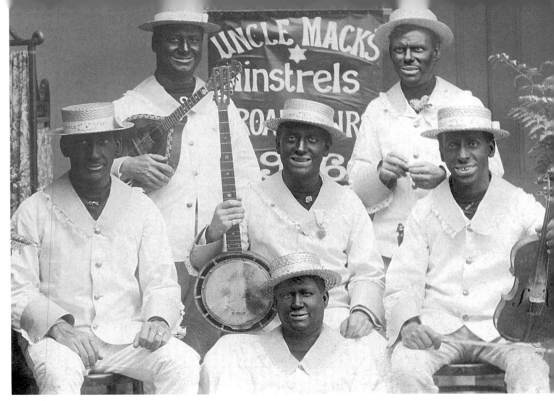

Uncle Mack and his Minstrels in 19
This postcard was taken in Thomas
Swaine's studio, situated in Broadsta
High Street. Uncle Mack retired at t
end of the 1948 season, and in
February 1949 both he and his wif
died.

A Swaine studio portait of the Guvr
Uncle Mack was an accomplished b
picker, and he could set people's fee
tapping and children clapping with
music.

Mr Dave Hall's Merry Mascots. These dandies
appeared for one year at Broadstairs Sands,
1905. Afterwards Mack was back! What
happened to these entertainers is a mystery.

Walter Dowling depicted as a merry jester.
I have no information about this entertainer
other than the photograph.

An art-deco style postcard of The Euterpeans, a vaudeville act. They were managed by Mr Wilson James under the direction of Percy Watson. This company appeared at Broadstairs Bandstand in 1910. They are Percy Watson, Miss Edith Payne, Alfred Wood, Herbert Spalding, Miss Marge Barras and Wilson James.

Mr Austin's Imperial Concert Party. These entertainers made regular appearances on Louisa Bay S accompanied by the small portable harmonium depicted in the background. They provided their coloured lamps, seen here hanging on the two uprights at either end of this miniscule stage. This lasted a number of years before disappearing into obscurity.

The famous thespian Maurice Farkoa, depicted here on a Swaine postcard. He first appeared at the Apollo Theatre, London, with Miss Edna May. His most successful role was as Viscount Gaston in *The Gaiety Girl* at the Gaiety Theatre, London, in 1896. He later appeared at the Bohemia, Broadstairs. He was born in France and was of Algerian extraction.

A Thomas P. Swaine postcard of Edward's Entertainers, a concert party that also appeared on the Lou Bay Sands. Notice the token female member of the troupe and also the baby grand piano.

Victoria Parade before 1905. The bandstand built by McFarland's and erected in 1895 stands in its original position, against the road. To the right of the bandstand can be seen the entrance to the Waterloo Steps. The bandstand was later moved to the centre of the Promenade in 1905.

This bandstand was the venue for Edward's Entertainers. It was located in the centre of the Promenade. The structure was made of ornamental cast-iron mouldings bolted together, so it could be moved. The bandstand lasted until 1952.

Mr John Wilson, Broadstairs bandmaster. He was also Bandmaster for the Queen's Own Oxfordshire Hussars, and for the Alexandra Palace Band.

In 1905 and 1906. John Wilson's Palace Military Band was part of the entertainment at Broadstairs Bandstand.

This is the Bohemians concert party which started in 1895. It first appeared on the small green opposite the Balmoral Hotel in Albion Street. The Bohemians were employed by the Balmoral management to entertain guests staying at the hotel. Sadly, the only names known are, from left to right, James Avon, Robert Denant and Tom Clare.

The entrance to the new Bohemia, 1905, previously known as The Lawn. It was renamed after the Bohemian concert party. The left hand post depicted here still stands today, and will be 100 years old in 2005.

7

Broadstairs Town

A Thomas P. Swaine postcard of an old print of York Gate, showing its poor condition before it was repaired by Sir John Henneker Bt, at his own expense. Originally known as Flint Gate, it was renamed after the Grand Old Duke of York. To the right, the mast of a ship can be seen in White's Shipyard. The sign hanging in the centre of the gate is for the Bell Inn, which is the building depicted to the right of the gate.

The York Gate, 1890s. By now fishermen's houses have been built to the left of the old gate, and the Bell Inn is now York Gate House. York Gate House was later to become a private school and then became a holiday home for Sir Francis Lakeing, Royal Physician to King Edward VII.

The Albion Hotel in Albion Street consists of three different buildings dating from various times, the earliest of these being the Phoenix public house. Under the ownership of Mr Ballard, the Albion was to have the pleasure of Charles Dickens's patronage, and at a later date Oscar Wilde visited for one night on 3 September 1888.

The Albion Hotel viewed from the sea, 1906. This is a picturesque view of Broadstairs' oldest and best-known hotel.

ckens House is now a museum and holds many surprises. The house is, in fact, two cottages. The lest part of the structure on the right hand side where the parlour is located is thought to be Tudor. e arch in the passage on the ground floor was the front door, and the cottage frontage faced mpston. The left hand cottage is thought to date from the reign of King James II or Queen Anne. The use was refronted in Georgian times and the balcony seen here is Victorian. The last private resident the house was Miss Gladys Waterer, who left the house to Broadstairs & St Peter's Urban District uncil. The curator of the museum today is renowned fashion historian Lee Ault.

The old Assembly Rooms on the Parade, once known as Nuckles Place. Later the house of Miss Crampton, it later became the Broadstairs Club, then Andersons Café. It is now incorporated into the Charles Dickens public house.

The Parade, Broadstairs, on a busy day. In the background is the Jubilee Clock Tower, but more interesting are the bushes and railings to the right and centre. This is where the Waterloo Steps, which led to the beach, were sited. They no longer exist.

The Jubilee Clock Tower was a gift to the town by R.H. Marks, MP, JP in celebration of Queen Victoria's Diamond Jubilee, 1897.

A Thomas P. Swaine postcard of an early print of Broadstairs. The date on the print is 1809 and the view is from the west. On the extreme left is Pierremont Hall, and in the centre of the bay is a mast for signalling, opposite Chandos Square.

Another print of Broadstairs at a later date, showing more housing along the clifftops. It also depicts shipping in the harbour and the old pier has taken on a more substantial look.

The same view as the previous postcard. This time the year is 1906, and the urban sprawl is beginning to show. Bleak House has been enlarged and Holy Trinity Church tower can clearly be seen.

These two images from a postcard by Thomas P. Swaine are from the same photograph as the previous card, although he has used artistic shapes to give it a different appearance.

This advert from the local newspaper, dated 29 January 1902, shows that Thomas P. Swaine not only had a photographic business but also carried out framing, regilding and the restoration of oil paintings.

The Carlton Hotel, built in 1899, stands on the corner of Oscar Road and Victoria Parade. To the right are Chandos Square and Spero Court Hotel, now private flats. This unassuming hotel was the first building in Broadstairs to display the town's armorial coat of arms on its façade. It was here that the British Olympic team stayed in 1924 while training for the Olympic Games. Two of that team, Eric Liddle and Harold Abrahams, are forever immortalised in the film *Chariots of Fire*. What other small seaside town can boast being host to an entire Olympic team?

ove: A view of 37, 35, 33 and 31 Wrotham Road, 1905. *Below:* Wrotham Road showing nos 13 to
. 1, followed by a rear view of the Cintra boarding house, which faces into Victoria Parade. The name
rotham comes from Wrotham House, which once occupied the ground where the Yarrow Home was
ilt. Wrotham House was once the residence of Mr Richardson. The Yarrow Home is better known
lay as Thanet Technical College.

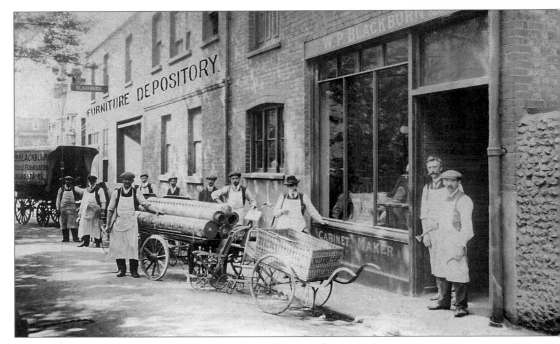

W.P. Blackburn's Depository and Undertakers in Buckingham Road, Broadstairs. The firm of Blackb[
provided everything a Victorian or Edwardian household needed. At 5 York Street was their bedding
furniture department. They were obviously major employers in the area, as there are twelve peop[
this postcard.

The interior view of Blackburn's shop in York Street. What would the TV programme *Bargain Hunt* r
of all this stock?

Another view of Blackburn's shop, which shows the considerable amount of stock carried. There was no 'just in time' policy here. As transport was by horse and cart or by hand barrow, holding extensive stock was a priority.

The phrase 'packed to the roof' applies to another view of Blackburn's. Mirrors and paintings adorn the roof space. Blackburn's business empire extended to Ramsgate where they had a shop in Kings Street until the 1960s. They also had a builder's yard in Oscar Road at one time.

Serene Place in Broadstairs High Street, *c.* 1900. It certainly lived up to its name when Thomas P. Swaine took this photograph. Note the large gas lamps suspended on the corner of the narrow High Street and also the large sign to the right of the building which has been 'touched out' by the photographer.

Milton Place almost directly across the High Street from Serene Place. It could only be accessed through a narrow passage in between two shopfronts, and was behind the row of High Street shops. It was built by the Culmers in the seventeenth century and demolished in 1910 when the High Street was developed and widened.

The Prince Albert inn with the London Central Meat Co. Ltd located to its right, *c.* 1912. The old Prince Albert public house was demolished in 1910, and this building was erected in its place. One of its more renowned landlords was Mr Barnaschina from New South Wales, Australia, who was nicknamed the Boko Poet of Broadstairs.

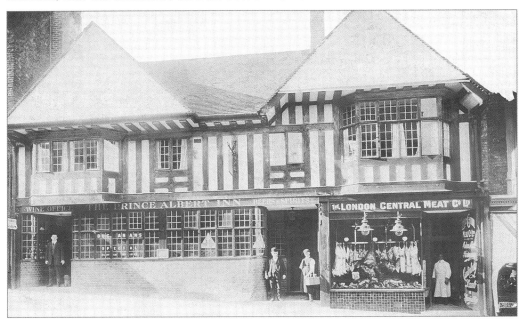

Prospect Place with the new Lloyds Bank on the right. The trees on the left once surrounded the open air venue called The Lawn. The site on which the bank was built was for many years a small farmyard, but when this was destroyed by fire the current building was erected.

The Majestic brake depicted here in Broadstairs High Street outside the well-known haberdashery establishment of Eveling's. The photograph was taken by Thomas P. Swaine while standing in Queen's Road. In the left hand foreground can be seen the Isle of Thanet tram lines that turn into the High Street. This three-horse-power transport was also used from Pegwell Bay to Minster.

Crofts Place, Broadstairs High Street. This photograph was taken on Sunday 30 July 1905 and depicts a parade organised by the Hospital Sunday Fund, whose headquarters were in the Railway Tavern (now Cramptons). Supported by all the friendly societies in the area, this parade was in aid of local hospitals.

Pierremont College private school was founded in 1907. The building dates back to 1785 and was a country seat for Thomas Forsyth; it was originally known as Pierremont House. From 1829 Queen Victoria stayed for a number of summer seasons. Notice the profuse vegetation.

Pierremont's grounds, 1904. It is hard to visualise 30 acres of woodland stretching from Pierremont Avenue to The Vale along the Ramsgate Road to York Street, then on to Belvedere Road and finally back to Pierremont Avenue, but this was the extent of the grounds belonging to Pierremont Hall. There were two gatekeeper's lodges, one in York Street and the other where the war memorial stands today.

Pierremont Mill, *c.* 1905. Owned by Mr. William Hills, the mill had stopped being used by the early 1900s and was demolished in 1909. The wooden shed to the right of the mill was used by Mr H. Goodburn to build vans and carry on the business of a carpenter and wheelwright.

Broadstairs station gates, leading to the High Street. From left to right the buildings are the Railway Hotel, Clarendon Road, Charles A. Childs offices, Cockett & Henderson's estate offices, the Railway Tavern and finally the Rennells & Childs office in Station Approach.

Mr W.H. White, the Honourable Secretary of the Broadstairs Fire Brigade, 1905. The Broadstairs and St Peter's Fire Brigade station was situated in St Peter's Park Road next to the Urban District Council offices, now the site of Broadstairs Library.

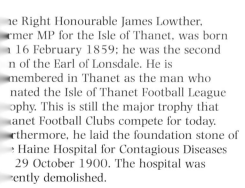

Four views of C.J. Elliott & Sons,
Monumental and General Masons, St Peter's
Park Road. C.J. Elliott later became Andrews
& Elliott Ltd, whose business today is in
Addington Road, Margate.

The Right Honourable James Lowther,
former MP for the Isle of Thanet, was born
on 16 February 1859; he was the second
son of the Earl of Lonsdale. He is
remembered in Thanet as the man who
donated the Isle of Thanet Football League
trophy. This is still the major trophy that
Thanet Football Clubs compete for today.
Furthermore, he laid the foundation stone of
the Haine Hospital for Contagious Diseases
on 29 October 1900. The hospital was
recently demolished.

The Isle of Thanet Football League Trophy, won by Broadstairs Football Club in the 1903/4 season. The cup was first presented on the 3 September 1899, and the first winners were Ramsgate Football Club, who beat St John's Guild. My thanks are due to Len Martin for this information.

The interior view of the Bradstow Lodge o the Freemasons, No. 2448. Mr W.H. White was the Lodge's Secretary & T.P. Swaine its Worshipful Master.

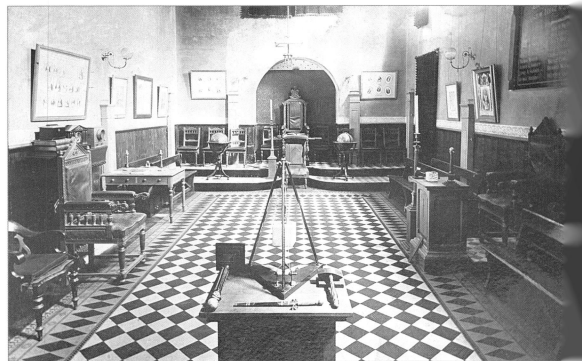

Queen's Road, Broadstairs, 1904. The three houses depicted here are nos 18, 20 (Glen Almond) and 22. The postcard was sent by Auntie Edie who lived in the middle house, no. 20. Today, 100 years later, this house still has the same name. The greenhouse at no. 22 has been replaced by a brick extension.

Queen's Road from The Vale, looking towards the High Street. Pierremont and King Edward Avenue had not been fully developed, and the trees on either side of the road were later to be felled to make way for housing.

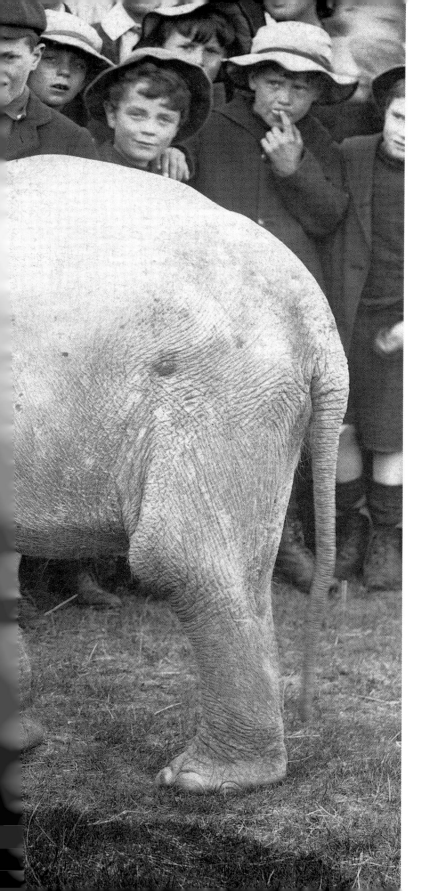

This is thought to be the Edge End field, when the circus came to town. I was told it was Barnum and Bailey's circus, and that the whole elephant troupe walked down Broadstairs High Street to bathe in the sea.

Granville Road, August 1908. The view is looking towards the Grand Hotel. Every house shown here still has its own walled garden. The age of the motor car was not yet upon us; today every front garden is used as a parking space.

No. 15 Granville Road, showing its wrought iron gate with the name of the house, Clovelly on it.

Riviera Mansions, 21 Granville Road, from the entrance to Louisa Gap. The photograph was taken after 1901, and shows a post that carried the overhead cables for the trams using the lower road route.

Glen Sannox is the third house on the left hand side of Pierremont Avenue at the Queen's Road end. Built in 1897, its first owner was Mrs Mindle.

Laurie House was situated at the Broadstairs end of The Vale. The Vale, once known as The Lynch, was the old track that led from Upton Farm to Goodson Stairs, later known as Louisa Gap.

No. 27 Westcliff Road, once known as Hannington House. In 1928 it changed its name to Sydenham and became apartments owned by a Miss Fuggle.

Kingswood, also in Westcliff Road, *c.* 1905.
t is situated on the corner of Seafield Road and
Westcliffe Road. This house has changed very
ittle over the last ninety-nine years. The house
on its left is depicted in the previous
photograph.

. 35 Westcliff Road in the early 1900s. The
ouse was named Mount View.

Still in Westcliff Road, this house is named Windermere. There is beautiful plasterwork above the attic window. Today this house is known simply as no. 45. The field in the foreground is the meadow on which the dairy herd of the Yarrow Home used to graze.

St Basil's, Westcliff Road, 1902. This house was next to the Lancaster Hotel. Sadly, both St Basil's and the Lancaster have been demolished to make way for modern flats.

The first houses to be built in Seapoint Road. The first three pairs of houses date from 1902. The open field in the foreground was the playing field of the Girls' School, known as Abbotsford, on the Western Esplanade.

The view to the rear of the Yarrow Home, *c.* 1907. This former children's convalescent home was built in 1895 with funds provided by the late Sir Alfred Yarrow, the owner of the famous Yarrow Shipyards. During the First World War the home was used as a military hospital, returning to its original use in 1919. The Yarrow grew its own vegetables and fruit. Its dairy herd was milked at its own dairy, situated where Yarrow Close is today.

Dumpton House School, 1905. The house faces West Dumpton Lane and was for some time a private school.

Dumpton House School, showing the spacious grounds that are now part of a housing development. The name Dumpton is derived from the ancient Dodemayton. The house is not far from Dumpton railway station and the current boundary between Broadstairs and Ramsgate.

8

St Laurence & Ramsgate

St Laurence High Street, *c.* 1906. This narrow road bears little resemblance to today's High Street. The buildings on either side of the road started to be demolished in 1938, and eventually the road was widened to three times the width seen here, but sadly it is still not enough for today's traffic. The third building on the left has a small sign on its corner, which tells us that it is the post office for St Laurence.

St Laurence High Street, *c.* 1910. The High Street had three public houses when this photograph was taken. The Rose Inn is on the left, where the Cobb sign is located. The building pictured in the centre background is the Wheatsheaf public house and on the right out of sight was the White Horse. It is interesting to note that two of the girls on the right are holding hoops, the classic toy of the day.

Ellington Park, 1904. Part of the Garret estate in 1866, before the estate was broken up, 12 acres were purchased by Edward Wilkie. In 1892 he sold the land to Ramsgate Corporation for £12,000.

Ellington Park, 1904. This view shows the rustic bridge and pond that once graced the park. Over the years much use was made of the park: among the events held by various societies were fêtes, open air concerts and floral fêtes. In later years a 'push ball' competion was run by the *Daily Mail* in the park, and in 1934 the Ramsgate Pageant, to commemorate fifty years of Ramsgate being made a borough, was enacted here.

Floral Fête, Ellington Park, 1905. Thomas P. Swaine captures this young lady's apprehension at being transported on this floral decked cart, holding her banner as well. If there is a driver on this cart, he or she can't be seen for flowers. What a pity that when this photograph was taken there was no colour photography.

St George's Church. This is the parish church of Ramsgate, consecrated by the Archbishop of Canterbury on 23 October 1827. In this same year an Act was passed which separated Ramsgate from the parish of St Laurence. Ramsgate became a borough in 1884.

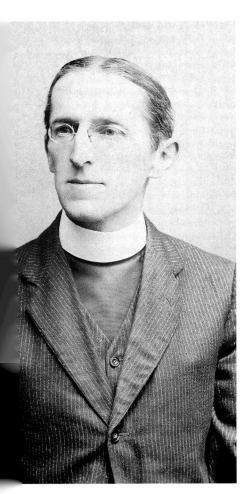

The Revd Leonard Jauncey White-Thomson, vicar of St George's from 1901 until 1907. He must have been a popular man as his surname was given to one of the school houses at St George's School. Leonard's son, Ian White-Thomson, was later to become Dean of Canterbury Cathedral. (*Information courtesy of Joyce Smith*)

Ramsgate Harbour, c. 1905. This view, taken from the western arm of the harbour, shows a busy day with many fishing smacks in view. Most of the fishing smacks seen here are of the small size (known as Toshers), which did not require the skipper to hold a Board of Trade Certificate. The larger smacks were over 25 tons and known as Dandies; a certificate was required to skipper these craft. The smack R168 is the *Gem* owned by S. Deveson.

Ramsgate Harbour, c. 1904. There is not much activity in this Swaine view of the harbour. In the middle wall, on the extreme right, is depicted one of a pair of sluice gates, which were used to scour the Harbour's silt. In the outer harbour is the old bucket dredger *Hope*. On the left can be seen the old fish market, which was blown up in the First World War.

The Harbour and Harbour Parade, 1903. With a magnifying glass one can make out, on the extreme right, the main entrance to the Royal Victoria Pavilion under construction; it opened in 1904. Among the buildings depicted on the left are Crampton's Hotel, Ballard, the draper, Orlandini, the confectioner, the Royal Oak Hotel, the Castle Hotel, the Alexandra public house and the Old Customs House. The smack in the foreground, R450, is the *Daisy* owned by Tom Hatton, the R149 is the *Meteor*, owned by A. Dyer and the R81 in the background is the *Skylark*, owned by F. Reeves.

The Quay Side, Ramsgate. This part of Ramsgate Harbour was where most goods were unloaded in the early days. Today the western end of the inner harbour has taken over this role. Some of the harbour's oldest buildings can be seen in this picture. On the right is the Clockhouse (now the East Kent Maritime Museum), built in 1871. The open space in front of the Clockhouse was once the site of many warehouses and the crane *in situ* is the only remaining clue of this area's former use. The building on the extreme right is the Isle of Thanet Ice Company's Warehouse, part of the Fish Market.

Ramsgate Harbour, *c.* 1905: a quiet day, with three private yachts moored to the quay. The first Harbour Master (Haven Master) of Ramsgate was Captain William Reed, appointed in 1751. His main duty was to hoist the Union Flag when there was 10ft of water at the pier head.

Ramsgate pleasure yachts, 1905. Seaside resorts such as Ramsgate and Margate were renowned for their pleasure trips. These short excursions were a lucrative addition to the local mariners' income and also gave the visitors a chance to test their sea legs. Because these vessels were all powered by sail, to gain the open sea and a sea breeze they had to be towed out by tugs. There were two paddle tugs at Ramsgate responsible for these operations: one was the *Aid* and the other was the *Vulcan*. This picture shows the tug *Aid* towing three pleasure yachts out past the Western Pier. From left to right they are the *Moss Rose*, *New Moss Rose* and the *Prince Fredrick William*.

Opposite: The tug *Aid* towing the *Moss Rose*. There was not much profit taken by the skipper of *Moss Rose* on this trip, with only five passengers on board. W. Allsup Ltd of Preston built the tug *Aid* in 1889 and she was registered in London. She was known to thousands of Londoners, none of whom set foot on her deck, for she was designed by the Board of Trade solely for harbour use and assisted the lifeboat with rescues in any weather. In 1915 the *Aid* was commandeered by the Admiralty to work out of Dover, and never returned.

The Royal Victoria Pavilion, Ramsgate. So much can be seen in this view. In the left foreground is the turntable belonging to the Sands station, then the rank of open carriages awaiting patrons from either the Pavilion or the station. In the far background is the *Aid* negotiating the harbour entrance, while the dredger *Hope* can be seen in mid-harbour. The obelisk on the right commemorates the harbour becoming a Royal Harbour by courtesy of King George IV in 1821.

Official opening of the Royal Pavilion. The Royal Victoria Pavilion was built to the designs of Mr S.D. Adshead and was opened on 29 June 1904 by Princess Louise of Argyll, here waiting to alight from her carriage. Ramsgate firemen form the Guard of Honour; their Captain, Mr West, can be seen facing the camera, standing against the Pavilion wall to the right of the entrance.

Thomas P. Swaine photographed these troops in Madeira Walk. They are mounted East Kent Yeomanry, who escorted Princess Louise to open the Royal Victoria Pavilion. The uniform they are wearing is what they would have worn four years earlier in the Boer War in South Africa.

The Sands and the New Pavilion. The stone groynes depicted here are now buried under sand that has been swept in by the tide. To the right of the 'Pav' can be seen the Sands railway station of the London, Chatham & Dover Railway, opened on 5 October 1863.

The Pavilion Sun Deck just after the Pavilion was opened. It was posted on 17 September 1904 to M
Chipperfield, 45 Nelson Street, Lowestoft, 100 years ago.

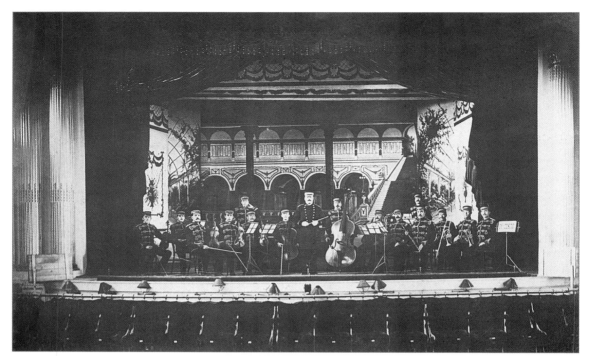

The Pavilion Band, 1905. This band can be seen in the background in the previous picture. Under the baton of Mr Maurice Wurms, these professional musicians entertained both inside and outside the Pavilion

The Royal Victoria Pavilion interior on the day it opened – a far cry from today's casino. Among the many artists to appear at the Pavilion was John Philip Sousa (1854–1932), the great American military musician and Al Tabor, a famous bandleader in the 1930s. The Pavilion was also a cinema and was the first to show Al Jolson's film *The Singing Fool*, the first talking movie.

Madeira Walk's waterfall and rustic bridge, 1904. This particular area was a photographer's haunt and many families had their photographs taken here by the numerous local photographers, including Thomas P. Swaine.

Madeira Walk, 1905. There was not enough room when Madeira Walk was built to install a long slope, so there was a short, steep, twisting incline – fine for horses and man, but difficult for the trams inaugurated in 1901. This postcard shows how close the trams were when meeting on Madeira's tortuous bends. The steep incline caused major and minor accidents, as the trams descended precariously to the harbour. Note the dress of the two gentlemen – the one to the right in a frock coat, top hat and cane, and the other in a bowler and three-piece suit.

Madeira Walk, c. 1905. Pictured here in its full glory, Madeira Walk was built by Pulham & So
from 1892 onwards, and officially opened on 6 April 1895. The cost was £60,000 but includ
other landscaping, including imitation rock gardens, a waterfall and a rustic bridge. The imitatio

one was, in fact, a mixture of cement and other ingredients sadly only known to Mr Pulham; it as known commercially as Pulhamite.

Madeira Walk, 3 August 1905. As mentioned before, the walk became synonymous with tram accidents. This picture shows the most famous of all. A tram, negotiating the first of two bends on its descent ran out of control and broke through the parapet on the left. It fell to the ground approximately 20ft below, but miraculously no-one was killed, although the driver was injured jumping clear. Even wet weather did not prevent crowds of sightseers from gathering to view the scene.

Albion Place, early 1900s. These fine houses were among twenty-six completed by 1792 in this area. Originally fences were erected in front of these buildings so that William Abbot could graze his cows on what is now Albion Gardens. One of these houses was St Martin's Hospital for Chronic and Other Patients (Women), with Sister Bethany in charge. In later years Ramsgate Borough Council offices were located here, along with the dreaded School Attendance Officer; in 1928 he was one Walter Hiram Baker.

Wellington Crescent, *c*. 1905. Construction commenced on these very elegant Regency buildings in 1817 once the former site of a Napoleonic period army camp and gun battery. The development was slow to start but by 1822 fourteen houses had been built. One of these elegant houses was the home of Sir Charles Warren, who was the Chief Inspector of the Police Force in Whitehall during Jack the Ripper's reign of terror. He later returned to the Army and led British forces in the Boer War.

Isle of Thanet tram accident, 26 May 1905. Not far from Wellington Crescent is the long road rising to Holy Trinity Church called The Planes of Waterloo. It was here that a no. 47 tram ran out of control while descending the hill. It could not negotiate the sharp bend at the bottom, and therefore ran off the rails into Vye's grocery shop. Fortunately no-one was killed, but the shop manager's 7 year old daughter and the crew of the tram received serious injuries. The tram had to remain embedded in the shopfront for a while as removal would have caused the shop to collapse.

Holy Trinity Church, Ramsgate, early 1900s. This church was built at a cost of £3,000 and flint and Caen stone were used in its construction. The church was consecrated by the Archbishop of Canterbury on 11 June 1845, and its first incumbent was the Revd John Gilmore. The builder was a local man, Mr W.E. Smith of Ramsgate. The church was named after an earlier Holy Trinity Chapel, which had been in Ellington Place.

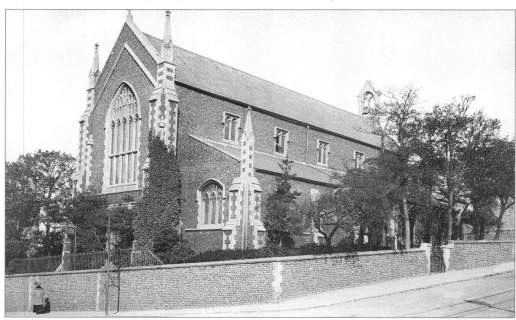

Paragon House Hotel, Ramsgate, 1905. This row of houses overlooks the harbour and sea, and was originally known during Wellington's time as St George's Fields. Most of the houses were built by 1816. The Paragon House Hotel on the corner was once the site of the Isabella Baths, built in 1817, later re-named Royal Kent Baths but they proved unprofitable and were therefore demolished. The present building was erected in 1864, and was known for many years as Mr and Mrs Rose's Boarding House. Vincent van Gogh lived for a short time not more than 100 yards away from this building.

Building the West Cliff Concert Hall. Beeching & Roses Shipyard can be seen in the background. Today's health and safety inspectors would be less than impressed with the lack of any safety equipment or precautions for this workforce!

Walking race, 1914. The contestants are passing the Paragon House Hotel. To the left and right is the chalk spoil from the site of the new West Cliff Concert Hall. There would soon be another need for digging, as Britain was about to go to war; hewing of trenches was to play such an important role.

Belgian wounded, 10 October 1914. This postcard depicts what was to become an all too familiar sight by the end of the First World War. Poor little Belgium had been overrun by the Germans and its brave wounded would be looked after in safety in England. Residences like the Granville Hotel and Lady Rose Weigall's home, Southwood House, were used as convalescent homes for this ever-increasing tide of torn humanity.

The East Kent Regiment, 'the Buffs', 1916. This photograph captures England's young soldiers in training to 'do their bit' for King and Country. This renowned cadet force were sadly being prepared for tomorrow's army, for the 'killing fields' of Flanders.

These four young cadets are nearing the time to enter their Battalion of 'the Buffs', 1916. The officer is unknown to me, but the NCO may be Sergeant Wren, who trained the Territorials at Wilson's Hall, Ramsgate. Both Thomas P. Swaine's sons saw service in France and India during the First World War.

This Beaulah & Swaine postcard captures a fish hawker somewhere in Ramsgate, not unusual for such a well-known fishing port. Obviously the word got out in the 'moggy' world, as Ramsgate felines follow this man's every step!

A postcard view of a house called Palma, 1 Brockenhurst Road, East Cliff, Ramsgate, March 1906. The two photo inserts are of Mr and Mrs George Wilson, the owners of the house. The message on the reverse reads: 'I send you Mr and Mrs R with a view of their residence. They hope to meet you some time during your stay here.'

St Augustine's Cross, Ebbsfleet, 1905. This Thomas P. Swaine postcard shows the cross that marks the spot where St Augustine landed in AD 597, where a well and an oak tree once stood. Legend has it that the oak grew from a staff that St Augustine pushed into the fertile soil of Thanet. Here Christianity grew like the oak in England. The stone Celtic cross was erected by Earl Granville to mark the spot in 1884.

9

Minster, Margate &
Other Places

Minster Abbey was founded in AD 670; the first Abbess was Domneva. It was later named St Mildred's Abbey after Mildred, the daughter of Domneva. The Abbey is one of the oldest continuously inhabited structures in the country. It was sacked by the Danes in AD 850 but was restored. In 1937 Mother Benedicta from Germany sought refuge from Nazi oppression and came to the abbey, refurbishing and restoring it as a convent of the Benedictine Order.

Montrose Ladies' College, *c.* 1905. This was a private college conveniently situated adjacent to the tramline from St Peter's Depot to Margate. The building is still there today and is now part of Lalem School. The tramlines can be seen in the foreground outside the college main gates, and continue round on to a private way linking Northdown Park Road and Northdown Road.

The Koh-i-Noor Restaurant, Cliftonville, *c.* 1905. A favourite with visitors and locals alike, when taking a cliff top walk in the early 1900s. Later this restaurant became better known as the Bungalow Café. The unusual name Koh-i-Noor comes from the very famous large diamond set in the Coronation crown, or perhaps from the paddle steamer that brought so many Londoners to Margate each season. After the Second World War the Bungalow Café was refurbished, but sadly was not economically viable. In 1980 it was turned into the Margate Aquarium, which was also a white elephant. In 1993 the site was cleared to make way for a car park.

Dane Park, Margate, covers an area of 25 acres. It was presented to the inhabitants of Margate by John Woodward in 1896. It took Margate Borough Council two years to lay out the park, which included a pond, a rustic bridge and a bandstand, along with various landscaping. On Wednesday, 1 June 1898 the park was officially opened by the Lord Mayor of London, Colonel H.D. Davies, MP. The reverse of this postcard is especially interesting as it was sent to Miss Newman, 124 High Road, New Southgate, by none other than Jessie Swaine, the wife of Thomas P. Swaine.

Endcliff Hall Hotel, 1906. This hotel was on the corner of Lewis Crescent and First Avenue, situated quite close to the sea; it was a busy and popular hotel in the early 1900s. Next to Endcliff on the extreme left is the Garfield Hotel.

The Oval, Margate, 1906. At the turn of the nineteenth century one of the most popular forms of entertainment at the seaside was military town or volunteer brass bands; it was not surprising that Margate had five bandstands. In the background are the Highcliff Hotel, Kimbers and the Queen's Hotel.

A closer view of the bandstand. This shows an intrepid duo entertaining a very attentive audience seated in tiered seating that formed a complete circle around the stage. In the background is Godwin Road, and the building on the right hand corner is Burlington Lodge. The Oval was built in 1904 but has now sadly been demolished: today the name Oval only refers to a grassed area.

Margate Harbour, *c.* 1905. This view is taken from the Imperial Hotel and shows a scene that long ago disappeared. To the left can be seen the pier and Droit House followed by the Ship Inn, behind which is the Metropole Hotel. All these buildings were demolished in the 1930s to clear space for the Fort Road dual carriageway.

The Slipway, Margate Harbour, 1906. Small wherries and fishermen cluster around the slipway while a no. 51 tram approaches Fort Hill. In the background are two of the oldest and most interesting building on the parade. To the left is the White Hart Hotel. Over 200 years old, it was the most popula commercial hotel in Thanet. Among its famous visitors were the Rt Hon. E. Gladstone, Prime Ministe and his famous political rival Benjamin Disraeli, MP, Earl of Beaconsfield. Next to it is the Royal Yor

...otel, converted into flats and shops in 1909 and named Royal York Mansions. It derives its name from ...atronage of Frederick, Duke of York, son of King George III. It also played host to none other than ...rince Louis Napoleon, nephew of Napoleon Bonaparte. After York Mansions is Duke Street, and on the ...pposite corner is Dunn's Parade Restaurant.

Margate from the lighthouse, 1905. Apart from the Droit House to the left, almost all the building
fronting the harbour were demolished in the 1930s clearance of Fort Hill. They included the Metropol
Hotel, the Ship Inn and Evelings, the drapers. The two tall chimneys in the background belonging t

obbs Brewery and Holy Trinity Church tower, covered in scaffolding, are sadly no longer landmarks of
d Margate. The Metropole Hotel deserves a special mention for it was here in 1929 that Sydney Fox
ommitted the most heinous murder of his mother.

Margate Harbour, 1905. This whole vista of the harbour and pier is captured by Thomas P. Swaine. In the distance a steamer is seen leaving the three-sided pier extension, added to the pier between 1875 and 1877. The Droit House shown here is the original, built during 1829. It was partially destroyed by the Luftwaffe during the Second World War and replaced with a near exact replica in 1947. On the extreme right is Marine Parade winding its way to Fort Hill, the scene of many tram mishaps during the early 1900s.

The three-masted *Tilikum* Canoe: the captain was John Voss, a Canadian mariner. Voss started out from Vancouver, British Columbia, in May 1901 and sailed 40,000 miles around the world. Sometimes accompanied by a companion (he lost one man in a tempest en route), he landed at Margate in September 1904 to an enthusiastic reception from local inhabitants. After much publicity this 2-ton vessel fashioned from a single tree was dismantled and shipped to London's Earl's Court for exhibition. In later years public spirited members of the Greenwich Yacht Club arranged for it to be returned to Canada, where it now resides in the Canadian Maritime Museum in Vancouver – a lasting tribute to an exceptional sailor.

Margate Pier, 1905. This view shows the twin life-boat stations and the pier extension that made up the pier complex. It was designed by the Pier Engineer supreme Eugenius Birch, and was constructed between 1853 and 1857. The pier was the first major project to employ Alexander Mitchell's marvellous invention of screw-piling. This consisted of screwing each pile that supported the pier into 10ft of solid chalk, and provided an immensely strong and stable base for it. Sadly the pier was partially destroyed during the storm of 1978, but it took a further twenty years before it was finally removed.

Pier extension, 1905. The pier extension was started in 1875 and took two years to build. During this time there was a loss in revenue to the Pier and Harbour Company and the town. On May Day 1877 the extension was officially opened by Sir John White, Lord Mayor of London, and proved to be a boon to all steamer captains. The extension was so popular that during the last week of July and first week in August 1877, 40,000 people paid *2d* each to use it, raising an income of over £6,000 for the Pier and Harbour Company.

Margate Marine Parade, *c.* 1905. This view is taken looking towards the Imperial Hotel at the bottom of Margate High Street. On the left hand corner of the High Street is Evans, the chemist, whose shops were

every Thanet town high street during the 1900s. Although the trams are running, brakes and
carriages can still be seen plying their trade along this thoroughfare.

High tide, Marine Parade, *c.* 1905. This scene depicts what Margate was all about – paddling ar enjoying the sunshine. As can be seen from the attire of the people, no one is wearing a bathi

stume, and most are wearing hats in the height of summer. Strangely, this card was not postally used til 15 December 1950, during the reign of King George VI.

The clock tower, *c.* 1905. The clock tower was handed over to Margate Corporation on 24 May 1889 having been built to commemorate Queen Victoria's Golden Jubilee in 1887. Depicted behind the tower in the background is Albert Terrace, originally called Hazardous Row because it was often affected by winter storms. In 1868 it was renamed, after Queen Victoria's husband.

Opposite: Lifeboat memorial, *c.* 1900. Placed on Marine Terrace, this memorial was erected in honour the eight lifeboat crew and one superintendent of Margate Ambulance Corps who lost their lives whe the surf boat *Friend of All Nations* capsized while answering distress signals from the vessel *Persian Emp* off the Nayland Rocks. The surf boat capsized only a few hundred yards from the shore, leaving on four survivors. This bronze statue of the lifeboatman stares out in vain across the Nayland Rock whe the disaster occurred, seeking nine brave lost friends.

Dent De Lion, *c.* 1900. Dent De Lion Gatehouse is situated to the west of Garlinge High Street and wa built in the reign of King Henry IV (1399–1413). It is all that remains of the ancient Dent De Lion mansion, of which the first kown inhabitants were the Sandwich family in 1248. Later Daundelyons a Pettits owned the mansion and during the eighteenth and nineteenth centuries it became a renowne pleasure garden and was also the site for Thanet races and games of cricket. Sadly, in 1888 a fir destroyed the mansion and farm building, leaving only the gatehouse, which is now incorporated into modern housing estate.

10

The Swaine Family

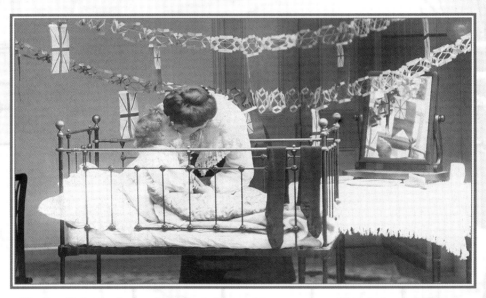

Thomas P. Swaine's daughter Doris featured in a number of his early postcards. As
you may have guessed, Doris is the little girl in the cot, and the lady giving her a
goodnight kiss is her mother, Jessie Swaine. The room is obviously Doris's bedroom
and is a unique peek into the Swaine way of living. The message on the reverse of this
postcard is in Jessie's handwriting, and is addressed to 'Miss E. Rolfe, c/o Mrs. George
Shrubsole, Bridge Street, Wingham' and posted on 21 December 1906. Doris was
4 years and 7 months old when this photograph was taken.

As mentioned in the introduction to this book, there is very little to add to the previous history of Thomas P. Swaine's only daughter, Doris Gwendoline Bertha, other than she finally married in later life a Mr Newman, and did not have any children. I make no excuse for including this fine portrait, taken by her father, of Doris as a young woman. She died at the age of 76 on 19 January 1978.

Ernest Horace Swaine was Thomas P. Swaine's elder son. At the beginning of the First World War he became a Special Constable in Broadstairs and later joined the Kent Cyclist Battalion. He later moved to Bedford and became an assistant in a photographic business in Watford, where he met his wife, Lily Margaret Sainsbury. In 1926 they had a daughter, Joan, who is the only surviving member of the family. In 1945 he divorced Lily, and moved back to Broadstairs, where he opened his own photographic business located at 80 High Street, his workshop being in Vere Road. His daughter Joan assisted in the shop until she too married in 1952. In 1959 Ernest married his second wife Audrey. After returning to Bedford, Ernest came back to Broadstairs to take many photographs of schoolchildren from St Laurence College, Ramsgate, and Stone House, Broadstairs. He died on 26 July 1962, aged 71. His daughter Joan and her husband Bob Ingledew still live in Bedford and have a daughter Diane and son Mark. Neither Joan nor Bob has any interest in photography.

An Ernest Swaine photograph of the Joy Wales School of Dancing at The Bohemia, High Street, Broadstairs, 1950s. Those of the troop pointed out to me are: Third row, Joy Wales (extreme left), Jean Day (fourth from right), Paddy Lacey (second right), Pat (third right), Daphne Mullins (fifth right); Front Row Ann Brazier (first right), Valerie Brazier (third right). The only boy present is Gordon Mullins. Many thanks to the Brazier sisters and Jean Day for their help in identifying these people and my apologies for not knowing the rest.

Ernest Swaine's Broadstairs High Street shop, as it was between 1947 and 1951.

Left: Albert Lewis Bradstowe Swaine, OBE, ED, aged 20. This is the second son of Thomas P. Swaine, born in Broadstairs on 25 October 1896, hence one of his Christian names, Bradstowe, which is the old name for Broadstairs. At the tender age of 16 he was already a member of the Territorial Army. In 1914 he immediately volunteered for Imperial Service on the Western Front. He was wounded at the Battle of Loos, and was then recommended for Officer rank which he took in 1917, serving in the East Kent Regiment, 'the Buffs'. After the war he went to Malaya to become a rubber planter. Then in 1942, as a Major commanding a Brigade of Signals, he was taken prisoner at Singapore by the Japanese Army, and spent the remainder of the Second World War incarcerated in Changi Jail. After the war he was awarded an OBE in recognition of his civic duties in Singapore and Malaya, helping this region of Asia return to its former stable democracy. Albert, affectionately known as 'Bertie', retired to Crowborough, East Sussex, where he subsequently died on 26 November 1983 at the age of 87.

Right: Stanley Eric Gordon Swaine, RAF Flight Lieutenant. This personal photograph was taken by his brother Ernest. Stanley was also born in Broadstairs, but on finishing his service with the Army, immediately after the First World War, he returned to Bedford to briefly work in the family business, and then joined the newly formed RAF in 1923, after his father's death. He naturally joined the photographic section and was seconded to take photographs of the early deck-landing trials on Royal Navy ships. The following photographs show some of his work while on board during his service career during both world wars.

Stanley's photograph of Sir Edwin Harris Dunning, DSC, RN, making the first successful landing on HMS *Furious*. Dunning was later killed on 7 August 1917 while carrying out similar landing trials.

The hazardous landing of aircraft on board the Royal Navy's ship HMS *Argus*, 10 July 1925. Depicted is Captain Alcock of the Royal Marines attempting to land a Blackburn Dart aircraft at a rather dangerous angle.

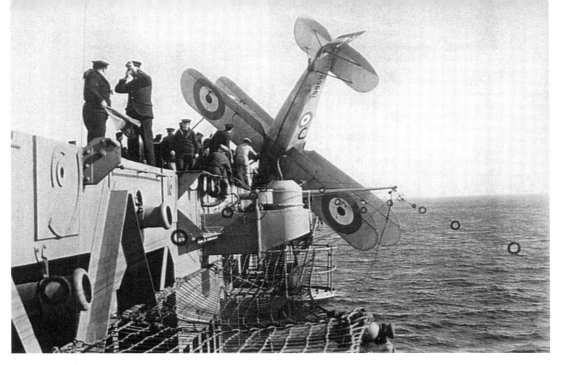

Flight Lieutenant Ridell crash-landing on HMS *Argus*, 30 January 1925.

When the Navy Takes Over the Air Force

BY LIEUT-COLONEL E. G. O. BEUTTLER

AN AEROPLANE LANDING ON THE DECK OF THE AIR-CRAFT CARRIER "ARGUS"

A humorous cartoon postcard by Lieutenant Colonel Beuttler depicting the trials of landing on HMS *Argus*.

Stanley Swaine's photograph captures Prime Minister Winston Churchill accompanied by Field Marshal Montgomery visiting frontline troops on one of their many morale-boosting tours.

Another of Stanley's photographs showing the pioneering pilots who during the inter-war years undertook deck-landing trials aboard a number of the Royal Navy's early aircraft carriers. They represent all three armed services, who risked their lives to perfect the art of landing aircraft on a moving ship's deck. On retiring, Stanley moved to Folkestone. He died at the age of 74 on 7 December 1972.

Jessie Swaine surrounded by some of her family, pouring afternoon tea in the garden of their home in Waterloo Road, Bedford, early 1920s. On the left her husband Thomas relaxes while next to him Jessie's mother, Fanny Box, waits sedately for her cuppa. On the right is young Doris, as yet unmarried, with her elder brother Ernest, who looks somewhat apprehensively at the camera – which must have been held by his younger brother, Stanley.

Thomas P. Swaine. This family photograph is possibly the last one taken of Thomas before he died of cancer in 1923. His life was colourful and never dull, although his family would probably have liked a more sedate and profitable lifestyle. Thomas lived life his own way.